I0470399

Creating Social Impact

How Your Firm Gains By Adopting a Socially Responsible Business Strategy

Pamela Cone, ISSP-SA

CONTENTS

CHAPTER ONE

The State of Corporate Social Responsibility

A worldwide shift is underway. We're on the cusp of a market movement around corporate social responsibility (CSR) and sustainability. While this has been a topic of interest for some time among more traditional sectors, professional service firms are realizing that robust programs around CSR and sustainability aren't just "nice to have," they're now a business imperative.

What exactly is CSR and sustainability? CSR, sometimes referred to more broadly as "social impact," is a company's commitment to manage the social, environmental, and economic effects of its operations responsibly—along with its goals of growth and profitability. In the most general terms, CSR deals with the role of business in society, with its basic premise that corporate managers have an ethical obligation to consider and address the needs of society, instead of acting solely in the interests of shareholders or themselves. Corporate sustainability strives to create long-term stakeholder value through business strategies that focus on the ethical, social, environmental, cultural, and economic dimensions of doing business.

CSR is an approach to doing business that benefits rather than harms society and the environment. Sustainability is a marker of a company's ability to survive into the future and eventually outlive its current owners. Corporate sustainability is often confused with CSR, and although the two are not the same, they are inseparably linked. While debate is ongoing about which of these phrases is the umbrella over the other, sustainability is a necessary, but not sufficient component of a company's CSR/social impact program and vice versa. One without the other constitutes an incomplete program.

Many corporate law firms are now asking themselves important questions about CSR and sustainability. How do we talk about it, how do we convey it, and how do we communicate the difference we're making in the socially responsible and sustainable space?

I've spent my whole career in professional services, with the first 15 years in the legal industry and the recent 15 years with Milliman, a global actuarial consulting firm. A large percentage of Milliman's clients are global and multinational insurance companies and financial institutions. Several years ago, we began to see very specific questions in requests for proposals (RFPs) from clients, including, "What is your firm doing with respect to corporate social responsibility and sustainability, and how are you measuring your impact?"

Like most professional service firms, Milliman participated in a wide variety of CSR-related initiatives, mostly organic, at the local-office level. These global offices all did different activities, but they weren't tracking them. The offices had no guidance. We had no strategic themes and no comprehensive, holistic story to tell. So, we just did our best to convey these efforts anecdotally when RFPs included questions about CSR.

For a long time, we did not give too much credence to these questions because we believed they did not really apply to us. While these questions might be important for other suppliers and vendors of the clients, for us—their trusted advisors—these questions did not seem so relevant. We weren't spewing metric tonnes of carbon out of smokestacks, dumping waste into the local river, or extracting resources from the earth.

The loss of a client

All of that changed in the summer of 2016. We actually lost an existing and important client in no small part because our answers on the CSR portion of an RFP questionnaire scored so low that our total score dropped below the threshold needed to make it to round two of consideration. It was an eye-opener. As the firm's chief marketing officer at the time, I dove into learning what was driving this increasing focus on CSR and sustainability by our prospects and clients. In part, the most obvious change was the sense of urgency, especially among insurance companies. Insurers are among the first to address the risks and costs of these social issues, not the least of which are climate change, poverty, floods, hurricanes, and fires.

Another noticeable shift is that a growing number of companies around the world are signing the United Nations Global Compact (UNGC). It signifies a commitment to the UNGC Core Principles on human rights, labour, environment, and anti-corruption, along with a commitment to take actions that advance societal goals, specifically the United Nations Sustainable Development Goals (UNSDGs) of 2030.

Goal 17 of the UNSDGs is "Partnerships for the Goals." It encourages partnerships of all kinds to help make greater progress toward the goals. That is one of the reasons why signatories of the UNGC are ensuring their supply chain and vendors are also committed to achieving the UNSDGs. Additionally, due perhaps to the current United States administration's decision to withdraw from the Paris Agreement, an increasing number of businesses throughout the United States have reaffirmed their commitment to make progress on climate change. In fact, companies and U.S. states are joining a Twitter campaign #WeAreStillIn. They're recommitting to their climate targets regardless of the United States' declaration to withdraw from the Paris Agreement.

As consumers, we often make purchases based on social impact practices and sustainability commitments of manufacturers, retailers, or restaurants. Employees or prospective employees are also forcing the agenda by asking employers, "What are you doing with respect to social responsibility? How are you measuring your social impact? What are you doing about sustainability? What does your diversity and inclusion program look like, and how are you measuring your progress?"

In the business to business marketplace, clients are influencing an increased focus on CSR and sustainability efforts of those they do business with. In the professional service industry, this increasing interest from clients and prospects may come as a surprise. While clients have always assessed the sustainability of their supply chain, professional service firms—law firms, accounting firms, and consulting firms—have enjoyed a somewhat protected relationship with their clients and have historically not been subject to scrutiny around CSR and sustainability policies, programs, and outcomes.

Today, CSR and sustainability programs are not optional. Increasingly, stakeholders are expecting all their vendors, suppliers, and employers to work toward greater social impact.

CHAPTER TWO

Growing Expectations of Stakeholders

Change is coming. Clients are driving improved social responsibility behavior of their service providers, much in the same way they have with other vendors in their supply chain. Finally, their attention is turning to professional service providers as well, thus changing the long-standing, cherished (and often protected) relationships with their lawyers, accountants, actuaries, and other advisors.

As early as February 2013, the Council of Bars and Law Societies of Europe (CCBE) issued a position paper entitled "Corporate Responsibility and the Role of the Legal Profession." This paper provides a very comprehensive snapshot of the state of corporate responsibility (CR) in the legal profession at that time and discusses the role of lawyers in advising clients in the CR arena. Interestingly, the paper cites attorney-client privilege as an advantage to serving their clients in CR matters and audits: "…the attorney-client privilege can provide critical benefit to their clients, for instance, when they are requested to audit their clients' compliance with legal and self-imposed CR standards."

The paper goes on to recognize the role of CR in law firms as "suppliers" to their clients and within the legal societies themselves. "It is, however, not only a new area of legal advice; law firms, bars, and law societies can also be subject to CR-requirements as "enterprises" and as suppliers of services, bound by CR requirements in their client's supply chain."

The CCBE report in 2013 noted that "some law firms have signed up to the UN Global Compact, a number of firms publish CR reports annually, a few follow the Global Reporting Initiative (GRI) guidelines, which contain key performance indicators regarding the Triple Bottom Line, or have adopted CR policies." It also goes on to recognize that a CSR program within a law firm may help with recruiting: "Finally, the adoption of sound CR policies may increase the attractiveness of law firms and enhance their ability to recruit talented young lawyers."

Firms face growing scrutiny

In April 2015, *Inside Counsel* featured an editorial "The Power of Good and Corporate Social Responsibility," that addressed the state of CSR in the legal industry: "Generally, most law firm programs have three components: pro bono and community service, diversity and inclusion, and sustainability. When treated as mere window-dressing or boxes to be checked, these concepts don't survive very long; however, when considered an intrinsic part of the firm's global strategy, each of these components, both individually and collectively, improves a firm's effectiveness and strengthens its brand."

The legal industry, in particular, will soon be subject to greater requirements and scrutiny by its stakeholders—employees, clients, prospects, and communities—with respect to CSR and sustainability programs. In a growing trend, businesses and government offices are employing in-house legal operations professionals to optimize delivery of legal services. This group's professional organization, Corporate Legal Operations Consortium (CLOC), is experiencing exponential growth. CLOC's website defines the profession as a multi-disciplinary function that optimizes legal services delivery by focusing on twelve core competencies.

Of the 12 competencies listed on their website, at least four lend themselves to driving change—strategic planning, financial management, vendor management, and cross-functional alignment. As CLOC professionals use their skills to drive desired behavior of their employers' outside law firms, they encourage and influence their outside service providers to meet certain criteria, whether it's alternative pricing models, innovative delivery, or social responsibility and sustainability efforts. With the general counsels' increasing reliance on their operations professionals for guidance on how to best manage their departments, CLOC professionals are in a unique position to affect desired change toward more robust CSR and sustainability programs and practices.

New expectations inspire change

The most prevalent example of how clients are successfully influencing their outside professional services firms to change is in the diversity and inclusion space. Clients, for quite some time, have been demanding that outside firms staff their projects with diverse teams in the professions, which historically (and accurately) have been described as "stale, pale, and male." This focus on diversity and inclusion in the legal profession is not slowing down. In fact, it is focusing even more on assessing actual progress (or lack thereof).

Given the successful pressure that in-house general counsels have used to affect change in their outside law firms regarding diversity and inclusion, they could and should use similar encouragement to ensure their outside law firms are serious about their social responsibility and sustainability programs. With the increasing adoption of and alignment with UNSDGs, client organizations will soon have "Partnerships for the Goals" discussions with their supply chain and vendors, including professional services providers. This will result in more private sector entities proactively engaging with the UNSDGs (and with each other) for the betterment of society. Will your firm be ready?

While some professional bodies and societies, particularly in the United Kingdom, have required professionals to "advance the public interest," corresponding professional bodies in the United State or Canada show little evidence of this.

While relevant social responsibility "thought leadership" is available from each of the professions, it seems as if it has been written and offered for "others" and not their own professions or their own firms. The cobbler's children, it seems, are barefoot!

It is becoming increasingly clear that firms can no longer coast through CSR questions and inquiries coming from stakeholders. At Milliman, the loss of an existing client because answers to the CSR portion of the questionnaire were insufficient to progress to round two of the process, conveyed a very clear message. It demonstrated the importance of CSR and sustainability to our client base, and we realized that we needed to transform our approach.

We realized, at a minimum, that we had to start tracking activities throughout the firm. The first thing we did was collect information about what each office was already doing organically. This allowed us to roll it up into firmwide totals. Clients are not asking just what one particular office is doing. They want a complete picture of what the entire company is doing and why.

Clarify roles and strategies

Historically, most professional service firms have assigned their office manager or HR manager the loosely-defined task of handling corporate sustainability or "community relations." Employees might establish a volunteer program, organize a donation drive for a food bank, or an executive or partner would encourage employee participation in a pet project. While all of these small actions have an overall positive effect, the resulting impact is comparatively small because they are unfocused and spread out across various causes. Today's consumers, clients, and employees are more discerning and want more well-executed CSR and social impact strategies.

In other industries, dedicated employees focus specifically on CSR and sustainability. Sometimes the social and community outreach staff are part of the Human Resources department. Diversity and inclusion is often part of HR, and sustainability and environmental footprint sometimes fall under operations or administration. For many companies, the job is multi-faceted and much bigger than one person can manage.

However, in most law firms, rarely is this a specific role, if it exists at all. More often, firms have staff devoted to a specific initiative, such as a pro bono program. Law firms also commonly have a diversity and inclusion initiative, largely because clients have started to require more diversity and inclusion in their law firms. Many law firms have a green team or committee dedicated to recycling or reducing waste. While having separate programs in various parts of the corporate structure is the current norm, market forces and stakeholders are all beginning to demand a more cohesive and comprehensive CSR and sustainability program.

Many law firms will resist the idea that implementing corporate-level CSR and sustainability practices is vital to stay competitive. Big corporate players may hesitate to allocate time and resources to CSR, seeing it as an expense rather than an investment. Unless they feel pressure from clients, most law firms won't voluntarily initiate a robust CSR/social impact program. The most visionary law firms, however, will recognize that a holistic CSR and sustainability program is a differentiator—at least for the short term—if they are proactive rather than just reactive. Eventually, however, this will become the standard.

Stakeholders today expect much more from all businesses, including law firms. On the consumer level, most people are more aware of and perhaps are making purchasing decisions based on the social impact or the sustainability practices of retailers or manufacturers. On the business-to-business level, stakeholders expect their businesses to do more, have a social voice, take a position, and use their skills and expertise to solve some of the most pressing social problems.

Fulfill your purpose and commitment

A great example of the increasing focus on sustainability can be seen in the annual letter to CEOs by Larry Fink, the CEO of BlackRock Investments. The last two years' letters have focused on sustainability. He states, "Unnerved by fundamental economic changes and the failure of government to provide lasting solutions, society is increasingly looking to companies, both public and private, to address pressing social and economic issues. These issues range from protecting the environment to retirement to gender and racial inequality, among others. Fueled in part by social media, public pressures on corporations build faster and reach further than ever before."

He also goes on to explain the importance of companies fulfilling their purpose and commitment to stakeholders and acknowledging the market forces that are causing change across many, if not all, industries. "Attracting and retaining the best talent increasingly requires a clear expression of purpose. With unemployment improving across the globe, workers, not just shareholders, can and will have a greater say in defining a company's purpose, priorities, and even the specifics of its business. Over the past year, we have seen some of the world's most skilled employees stage walkouts and participate in contentious town halls, expressing their perspective on the importance of corporate purpose. This phenomenon will only grow as millennials and even younger generations occupy increasingly senior positions in business. In a recent survey by Deloitte, millennial workers were asked what the primary purpose of businesses should be—63% more of them said "improving society" than said "generating profit."

Make client work part of your CSR strategy

Recently while on a Delta flight, I flipped through the airline's in-flight magazine. Three different articles discussed sustainability, fossil fuels, and what Delta is doing about their energy usage and their corresponding carbon footprint. They reported on how they're giving back and trying to be a better corporate citizen. I would like to think that these efforts by Delta are in collaboration with their outside law firms. Lawyers must see themselves as trusted advisors, helping clients address these business and societal challenges. The traditional law firm mindset has been to think of CSR as its pro bono program and not necessarily the everyday work it does for clients. The prevailing sentiment up until now has been that the work the firm does every day for clients is just that—work. They don't see that sometimes client work actually improves society. The future of CSR is to incorporate the firm's identity and the work it does for paying clients into its sustainability goals. If Delta's law firm is helping Delta navigate its commitment to reducing its fossil fuel usage, it could fit with the law firm's own CSR strategy, as well as their client's, all while maintaining the revenue stream from that client and meeting both organizations' needs.

Who better to address some of these pressing challenges facing society than the esteemed legal profession? This profession is educated and extremely intelligent. Attorneys know regulations and how to pass legislation. The profession knows how to form public-private partnerships. We should lead this mission, not just sit at the table. Unfortunately, right now, attorneys aren't even at the table, even though the legal industry is so well-equipped to take on this work.

CHAPTER THREE

Telling Your Story Holistically

As demand grows for ethical and sustainable practices, you'll benefit by embracing CSR and sustainability as an integral part of your firm's culture. If you only engage in CSR for marketing purposes or to be able to "check the box," it's not authentic. If it's not genuine, your employees, clients, stakeholders, and your marketplace will quickly figure it out and respond accordingly.

We are reaching the point where CSR has to be something you *are*, not just something you *do*. It must be part of your corporate DNA. It has to be demonstrative of your values as a firm. If you can achieve this, it will be authentic. The goal is for CSR to represent the core of who you are as a firm.

As an example of the distinction between an actual CSR strategy and simply "doing things," a yearly coat drive for homeless families at holiday time is a kind thing to do, however, unless this action aligns with your corporate vision, it isn't part of the whole company's identity. Your company's CSR approach should reflect your firm's themes, values, and vision.

The firms that are doing this well are no longer treating CSR as a side project separate from the firm's executive management team. Embedding CSR and sustainability into your business model is now the expectation. The business framework of the future will require firms to include sustainability and social impact practices into the way they operate. A CSR program should not exist to "undo" the damage the business is doing, but rather to conduct business in a more sustainable manner from the start. CSR should be considered and incorporated into every strategic business decision.

One of the biggest challenges for firms is to uncover the firm's core values. Many corporate law firms have simple mission statements along the lines of, "We strive to provide high quality, top-end legal services to our clients." These sorts of mission statements are not specific enough to differentiate your firm from competitors, nor are they specific enough to delineate a clear path for CSR and social impact.

Find your firm's DNA

The first step to creating a CSR strategy is to examine your firm's culture and values at the highest level. Since this initiative needs to permeate the entire company, the best place to start is at the top. A robust CSR committee should not only include administrators who can enact programs and communicate with the rest of the firm, but also board members, executives, and members of the governing body. When possible, involve stakeholders, clients, and vendors for input as well. Find out what is important to them, what causes they support, and how your firm and its strategy can reflect their CSR goals.

Once you've assembled all the important parties, work to focus your efforts and initiatives. What is your organization's mission statement? What is your company's vision? What are the values of your firm? These are crucial questions when considering how to design your CSR initiative, and the answers should inform your strategy.

For example, global actuarial firm Milliman's mission statement is "to work with our clients to protect the health and financial well-being of people everywhere." As an actuarial consulting firm, this mission accurately and succinctly describes the difference it strives to make in the world through its work. The firm's CSR strategy is comprehensive and organized by a committee, which includes the chairman, CEO, and COO. This ensures that CSR and social impact program activities align with and support the firm's overall strategy.

Create a holistic strategy

While some companies may assign programs to different departments (i.e. diversity and inclusion may fall under HR, or perhaps a director leads your pro bono program), it's imperative that these all align with your firm's overarching values and are included in its overall CSR story and communications. The firm's approach to CSR should be *holistic* as stakeholders, employees, future employees, clients, prospects, and the communities where you operate all expect CSR work to align with the firm's brand, skills, and expertise.

Currently, most professional service firms don't have a cohesive CSR strategy. Social impact activities are organic and random, as each office makes decisions locally. It may be a challenge for service firms to integrate sweeping changes because they fear being dictatorial, and that mandating decisions from the top will deter offices from feeling invested in the program. One way to encourage participation is by surveying stakeholders, employees, partners, and even alumni and retirees of the firm. Ask them, "What would you like the firm's social impact themes to be? Would you like our efforts to focus on the countries where we have offices, or should we focus globally?"

Stakeholders expect you to think holistically and embed CSR and sustainability into the way you conduct your business today. That means that service firms need to consider the type of work they do for their clients. Is that work contributing to the firm's CSR goals? If your firm is aligned with the UNSDGs, is your CSR program contributing to those goals? And is the work you do for clients contributing to the UNSDGs?

Most firms don't consider the work they do for clients as part of their social impact story. A broader view is in order. For example, in Milliman's case, a climate resiliency team works with clients to help them understand and address the ramifications of climate change. That client work makes progress toward the UNSDGs and fits with the firm's mission of "protecting the health and financial well-being of people everywhere." This work is part of Milliman's social impact story even though it's not considered pro bono work.

In many law firms, especially the large global and multinational firms, separate leaders and separate departments address pro bono, diversity and inclusion, social responsibility, and a volunteer green team. In that case, one hurdle will be to think holistically to paint the picture of overall social impact for stakeholders, combining the results and stories of all these initiatives into one comprehensive social impact story. This approach conveys the efforts of the firm to make the world a better place—and ideally includes the work done for clients to help address the most pressing societal challenges.

Align with like-minded clients

Goal 17 of the UNSDGs encourages companies to examine their supply chains and vendors. Are their values aligned with yours? Are they also striving to achieve the goals? Are they also trying to make the world a better place, or is the business actually doing more damage than good? If so, how can their law firms help them pivot to a more sustainable business model? After all, if a law firm's clients are conducting business in a non-sustainable manner, or they're in an industry that isn't sustainable, the law firm will eventually lose those clients as they go out of business.

CHAPTER FOUR

Align with a CSR Framework & Industry Organizations

It can be quite an undertaking to build and institute a CSR program focused on corporate and environmental sustainability. After deciding how to align your program with your organization's unique mission and purpose, a second step is to align your company with external associations and industry bodies to reinforce and support your comprehensive CSR program and strategy.

The UNGC and corresponding UNSDGs are the most well-known and favored framework that is emerging as the standard throughout the world

The UNSDGs consist of 17 goals that are considered the blueprint to achieve a better and more sustainable future worldwide. As explained earlier, the UNSDGs address global challenges, including those related to poverty, inequality, climate, environmental degradation, prosperity, peace, and justice.

When companies become a signatory to the UNGC, they're committing to the 10 principles of the Global Compact as well as committing to making progress toward the UNSDGs. As a signatory, you're expected to report progress annually through a Communication on Progress or COP. Goal 17—Partnerships for the Goals—encourages us to reach out to clients, third parties, nonprofits, and public and private entities so that together we'll have a much greater impact than any single entity could achieve alone. Specifically, two of the underlying targets of Goal 17 read as follows:

17.16 Enhance the global partnership for sustainable development, complemented by multi-stakeholder partnerships that mobilize and share knowledge, expertise, technology, and financial resources, to support the achievement of the sustainable development goals in all countries, in particular developing countries.

17.17 Encourage and promote effective public, public-private, and civil society partnerships, building on the experience and resourcing strategies of partnerships.

While the financial commitment may dissuade some companies from formally signing the UNGC (although for most law firms, this should not be a deterrent), you can still align your company's actions with that framework. The UNSDGs have quickly become the common language that people understand. More than that, UNSDGs are now being included in elementary, high school, and college curriculums all over the world.

With a target date of the year 2030 and a great deal of companies striving to make progress, expectations from consumers are higher than ever. Referencing the UNSDGs in your firm's communications around CSR and social impact programs will immediately help your stakeholders understand the components of your program.

Understand what your clients value

With external alignment, it's important to understand your clients' values to help align collaborative efforts with your firm's values. For instance, a real estate firm that primarily works with real estate developers as clients should consider joining a body dedicated to sustainability issues for real estate developers. For a global firm that has 37 practice areas and works with 16 different industry bodies, it would probably be more beneficial to align with something broader like the UNSDGs.

You'll immediately resonate with your audience if you use the framework to focus your efforts and shape your communications. For example, if a law firm talks about its commitment to tutor in local schools, it would be considered a very good thing. However, if it talks about tutoring in local schools because it is striving to make progress toward United Nations Goal 4, Quality Education, it's using the common language that most companies now understand, as the UNSDGs permeate society's efforts around social impact.

The beauty of the UNSDGs is that each firm can choose the goals that are most material and relevant to them (and their clients). You don't have to try to make progress on all of the goals because not all of the goals are going to be in your sweet spot. Using Milliman as an example, it can do little as an actuarial consulting firm to contribute to the "Life Underwater" goal. However, actuaries can contribute greatly to goals that achieve quality education, quality healthcare, improved infrastructure, and sustainable cities, to name just a few.

Explore the industry bodies your clients belong to around this topic that are relevant to your corporate values. For law firms, you'll find the Law Firm Sustainability Network in the United States and the Legal Sustainability Alliance in the UK. Other bodies include the Sustainability Accounting Standards Board, the Principles for Responsible Insurance, Principles for Sustainable Investments, and even a banking sustainability group called Sustainable Banking Network. Your clients may already belong to an industry organization, and you should join them to help address the issues affecting their industry.

So, what is the benefit of joining these organizations or associations, such as the Law Firm Sustainability Network? Well, specifically, you can understand what other law firms are doing. You can access their benchmarking tools. You can see how your firm's performance compares to your peers and share best practices. If you're not even a member of your own industry's sustainability organizations, it could call into question your claims about the good sustainability work you're doing with clients.

Choose projects that match your expertise

Law firms and other professional service firms should choose social projects that align with their skills and expertise. It doesn't make sense to put hammers in lawyers' hands and expect them to build a high-quality house for Habitat for Humanity. While Habitat for Humanity is a wonderful program doing great work, these types of CSR initiatives don't leverage the best and most useful skill set of your lawyers. Instead, consider working on initiatives that leverage the highest and best talents of your people.

One example is provided by Nixon Peabody. The environmental and energy lawyers at Nixon Peabody formed a nonprofit with clients that produce solar panels, clients who are real estate developers, and the District of Columbia to place solar panels on the rooftops of municipal and office buildings in the District. All of the generated energy is being credited to low-income housing in the District. This is a great example of using your skills and expertise to partner with others to create a lasting and sustainable social impact.

For an example outside the legal industry, consulting firm Milliman employs brilliant actuaries, computer scientists, and data scientists, among many other technical and business professionals. It would make little sense for them to volunteer their time building homes or pulling weeds in a local park. The strength of their human capital lies in the ability to understand numbers and manage future risk. Therefore, Milliman recently partnered with Math Motivators, a program of The Actuarial Foundation, to tutor local, underserved high school students throughout the United States. This program aligns perfectly with both the skill set and corporate values of Milliman, and it clearly contributes toward UNSDG Goal 4 - Quality Education.

CHAPTER FIVE

Match Your Social Impact Programs with Your Mission

Most firms' offices are already involved in their community through volunteering, charitable giving, or board service. Most firms already have implemented some sustainable programs in their offices, like recycling, or they work in a LEED certified building. However, if you want to take your CSR and sustainability program to the next level, you can have greater impact by focusing that variety of activities and initiatives under some theme umbrellas that fit with the culture and the mission of your firm.

One strategy is to align your CSR and sustainability programs with your mission or vision statement. If you don't have a firmwide mission or vision, you may want to start by working with your governing body or crowd-sourcing what your themes should be. You can hold focus groups of employees and partners in person or conduct a firmwide survey. One of the biggest mistakes firms make in this step is that they don't include all of their stakeholders, including staff, associates, partners, retirees, alumni, and clients, and perhaps community members with whom the firm has a good relationship.

Ideally, the process should elicit what your stakeholders feel are the top two or three themes around which you should build your program. If your firm also has a foundation or some sort of philanthropic giving body, the themes should be aligned to guide both programs. In other words, you should not have themes for your CSR and sustainability programs that are different from the themes for your giving program.

Again, in Milliman's example, it surveyed all of those stakeholders that I described and asked what they would like CSR, sustainability, and giving programs to focus on. Three themes clearly emerged, which were:

> 1. Education in the STEM categories particularly in underserved schools

2. Public, global, and mental health services and access to those services
3. Community investment and engagement, particularly where it includes job creation

You may also want to ask your stakeholders, "Do you want our programs to focus only on the cities or countries where we have offices, or should our program be more expansive or global in scope?" At Milliman, the answer came back very clearly by a two to one margin. Those queried felt that the program should be global in scope.

Firms should also look at and assess the work they're actually doing for clients. How does client work fit under these identified themes? Firms often forget to talk about the actual business they're conducting as part of their CSR commitment or the efforts they're making in the sustainability space. They should look at the entire picture, including the work clients are paying them to do. Firms should ask themselves these two questions:

1. Is our client work complementary and aligned with our social impact themes?

2. Is our client work contradictory to our social impact themes?

Stage one of communicating your strategy with stakeholders is engaging them to help identify your CSR themes. If you enlist their input, they're more likely to embrace the outcome. After you have identified your themes, it's advisable to wait until you have specific examples of how you're achieving your goals, including measurable results, before you celebrate your themes externally.

CHAPTER SIX

Transactional vs. Transformational Impact

The maturity stages of a CSR program generally fall into three distinct tiers: transactional, transitional, and transformational. Traditionally, CSR involves the three Ts of philanthropy: time, treasure, and talent. With transactional programs, we mostly give treasure, perhaps a little bit of time, but rarely specific skills or talent.

Historically, firms have done "stuff" which I refer to as "random acts of kindness." Perhaps it is something the local offices have organized or a cause that key partners are interested in. All are really good things. I refer to these things as "transactional." Transactional programs are usually *local*, *unorganized*, and *unfocused* and don't necessarily fall under the company's CSR themes and values. That doesn't detract from the good that they are doing, but a greater impact could be made with more organization and collaboration both within the organization and with external parties.

The next level—transitional programs—are where the firm might identify two to three themes and give corresponding guidance to the local offices and practices. The firm recommends aligning or finding programs under these three themes that their stakeholders identified. While this approach offers guidance, it still leaves the decisions to the local practices. Usually in the transitional stage, firms are giving treasure, time (i.e. volunteered time), and perhaps some talent—aligned with the identified themes.

In the transformational stage, a firm identifies broad projects that many people throughout the firm can participate in, along with third parties, whether they're clients or other public or private entities, nonprofits, or NGOs. During this stage, the firm has developed programs or is collaborating on programs that are truly transformational and provide a transformational outcome because of the collaboration.

Transformational initiatives consist of time, treasure, and talent, and the corresponding impact is much greater than what any individual office or firm could achieve alone. The example given earlier of Nixon Peabody working with solar panel clients, real estate developer clients, and the District of Columbia's public housing to generate electricity for low-income tenants is a wonderful example of a truly transformational social impact program.

Expand your social impact reach

In order to move from transactional to transitional to transformational, a firm must have and demonstrate support from the top, because if firm management isn't interested in seeing CSR and sustainability programs mature, then the path from transactional to transformational will be difficult. Stakeholder pressure, whether it's from clients, employees, the community at large, or just the expectations of businesses today, will likely be the biggest driver for firms to go from transactional to transformational.

One other point to consider when aspiring to go from transactional to transformational is understanding the difference between spreading your resources across a wide range of transactional one-off activities or focusing resources and collaborating with others to strive toward truly transformational outcomes. For instance, many law firms now list a wide range of activities on their websites. All of them are great initiatives, but they don't fall under a cohesive mission or theme. The result is a series of small impacts rather than larger, transformational changes.

It is vitally important to note that these three phases of social impact need not be mutually exclusive and, in fact, rarely are. Most firms have initiatives in all three stages. In other words, just because a firm may launch a transformational program firmwide does not mean all initiatives already underway at the transactional or transitional phases must cease. Initiatives in those phases may very well continue advancing along the continuum to maturity.

CHAPTER SEVEN

The Time for Change is Now

As service firms begin to ponder the power of having an effective and comprehensive CSR strategy, they may be asking themselves why? Why should law firms embrace CSR and strive to reach the transformational level.

The simple answer is that law firms should care because their clients care. Their clients expect that law firms are poised to help them address these challenges. Law firms need to care in order to be trusted advisors to their clients. Clients also expect law firms to exhibit these good practices too. If not lawyers, then who? The legal industry has the expertise to navigate these immediate challenges.

There was a phrase that we used to practice in typing class when I was younger (I know, I am dating myself here!) because it used all the important keys on the typewriter. "Now is the time for all good men to come to the aid of their country."

I often use that sentence when I speak about the importance of CSR. I change it slightly to include both men and women and to encompass the entire globe, but I think it beautifully captures the essence and the importance of this work.

"Now is the time for all good men and women to come to the aid of their world."

CSR is not something that can be ignored. We see daily examples in the news about the drive to create a more sustainable and just world. These problems aren't going to go away, and they're not "future" challenges. They are "right now" challenges.

I firmly believe that the world is depending on those most capable to lead this change. That, in large part, means risk management and legal professionals because they understand the legal implications and ramifications. They are most equipped to assess and mitigate the risks of continued "business as usual" for clients. They understand the regulatory environment, the legal terms on an international stage, and associated risk management. If companies that law firms represent can't figure out a way to survive long-term, law firms are not going to have clients to represent in the future.

Service professions, in general, are hired to manage risk and be trusted advisors to their clients. For decades, law firms have talked about striving to be trusted advisors to their clients. They continually work to "add value" and to be innovative in helping their clients' businesses. Being a trusted advisor means looking beyond the legal sphere and helping clients navigate their overall business issues, which includes social impact, sustainability, and survivability into the future.

Right now, smart companies are making plans or are already pivoting to ensure their business models are sustainable. Those that aren't are just riding the tide until there's no more tide left. However, CSR and sustainability are not issues we can ignore. Our future is not something we can wait to address. We must act now to make sure we have a future at all.

There is no Planet B!

Services and guidance for your firm

Are you ready to create or refine an existing social impact strategy? I can help you:

- Identify and aggregate your social impact programs
- Audit current efforts and identify gaps
- Set goals and create a strategic plan
- Communicate your social impact strategy with clients, employees, and senior leaders
- Execute your plan
- Measure progress

For a complimentary consultation about your firm's strategy, contact me:

pamelacone@amityadvisory.com

206.499.6890

ACKNOWLEDGEMENTS

I want to express my sincere gratitude and thanks to the people in my life who have encouraged and supported me personally and professionally, especially my husband Patrick, who kept the home fires burning during my global travels over the last 30 years, and to our son, Ian, who is the reason I am striving to make this world a better place. Together, we three are quite a team.

And a huge thank you to my mother with whom I only had 17 years, and to my father, whose guidance I still call upon to this day. Without their high expectations and unwavering encouragement, I would not have developed the fearless desire to grab every opportunity and experience available to me. Thank you for making it the norm, not the exception.

ABOUT THE AUTHOR

After nearly 30 years of launching, building, and developing marketing, communication, and business development programs in professional service firms, often against all odds, Pam felt compelled to do it one more time. This time, she is focusing on Social Impact and the role professional service firms and their clients can and should play in this movement.

Her studies in international relations in college and graduate work in communications management and corporate social responsibility and sustainability, along with decades of professional service firm experience have prepared her for this focus. Pam is now leveraging her highest and best skills to help ensure that service professions—lawyers, accountants, actuaries, and engineers—are leveraging their highest and best skills to address and solve the world's most pressing challenges.

Pam is the founder and CEO of Amity Advisory—a social impact consulting firm for professional service firms. She and her husband split their time between the Northwest and the Midwest United States. Their son, Ian, is working on his graduate degree at Rice University in Houston, Texas.

www.amityadvisory.com
pamelacone@amityadvisory.com
+1 206.499.68

TESTIMONIALS

"Pam has brought tremendous energy to her role leading the CSR program at Milliman. With her leadership, we have engaged employees across the firm to share their ideas and activities. She has inspired all of us to do more. Pam has focused on aligning our CSR goals with Milliman's mission. This has increased support across the firm and provides a consistent and positive external message. I am proud of Milliman's increased CSR commitment. Pam has been key in making this happen."

Stephen A. White, FSA, EA, MAAA
President and CEO
Milliman

"Pam did a tremendous job developing all aspects of our CSR program. Her energy, enthusiasm, and passion were on display from the initial discussions with senior leadership to the recruitment and training of our CSR Ambassadors. Thanks to her leadership, we have a program that our employees are proud to be a part of."

Bill Pedersen
Chief Operating Officer
Milliman

"Pam was instrumental in developing our CSR program and generating tremendous enthusiasm throughout the firm. Her insight in defining a program structured to build from the ground up has allowed our employees to contribute and feel tremendous pride from day 1. She has leveraged that structure to build a cohesive community around the globe, which has helped connect us in new and exciting ways."

Patricia L. Renzi
Principal – Life Technology Solutions
Milliman

"Pam brings a lot to the table with her breadth of experience in the CSR space. She's both insightful and thoughtful, bringing a practical approach and inspiring transformative action."

Gayatri Joshi
Executive Director of the Law Firm Sustainability Network
Vice President of EcoAnalyze